For my husband,
Kevin,
as it was before,
as it is now,
as it will be
into infinity . . .

Between Friends

Copyright © 2000 Lynne Gerard.
All rights reserved.
Originally published in the USA by C.R. Gibson
Company. This edition published by Eagle
Publishing, P O Box 530, Guildford GU1 4FH.
Typeset by Eagle Publishing.
Printed in Hong Kong
ISBN: 0 86347 394 6

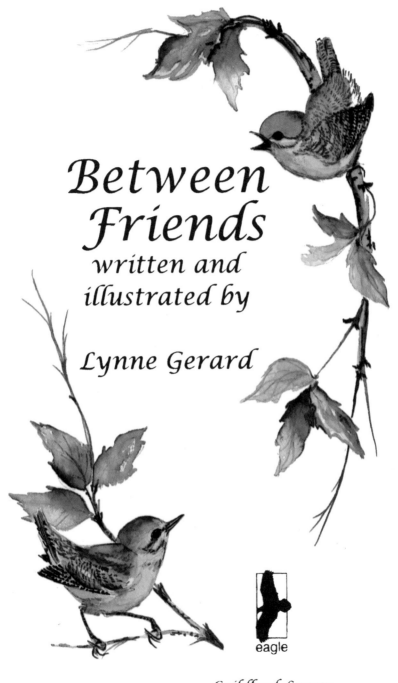

Between Friends

written and illustrated by

Lynne Gerard

eagle

Guildford, Surrey

A good friend
is like a rare shell
washed upon a
quiet beach.
One who discovers
such a friend
finds a priceless
gift from
God.

Having a
special friend
is a true blessing,
and
evidence that
you, too, are
special.

Friends help us
know ourselves a
little better,

*and like
ourselves a
little more.*

*Good friendships
enlighten the mind,
enrich the heart
and enhance
our lives
day to day, and
season to
season.*

Lynne gerard

*Friendship
is as necessary
as the sun, as
constant as the
stars and as
rewarding as
spring
after a
long winter.*

One does not
go out into the
world in search
of friendship . . .

friendship is something
that happens
naturally, when the
time is right, like
a rainbow in the sky.

The world is
as wide as the sky
and beyond,
and as infinite as
the twinkling
stars . . .

that two
kindred spirits
should come together
in friendship
is surely
evidence of
divine
intervention.

It is a fine,
divine wind that
carries a tiny
seed, just so,
and take it
to the very
place where
friendship
needs to
grow.

*Friends possess
something in
their character
that we
admire
and wish
to add to
our own
lives.*

There is an
honesty between
friends that is
rare to other
relationships . . .

*this is part
of the magic
of friendship.*

With a good friend,
there is
a comfort zone
like none other,
where sharing even
silence can be
a pleasure.

*The struggle to
make ends meet
in this busy,
complex world
often burdens our
hearts . . .
friendship
helps soften
the hard edge
of
life.*

*Good friendships
contain the strength
of affection
that makes
forgiveness instantaneous
and disappointment
forgotten.*

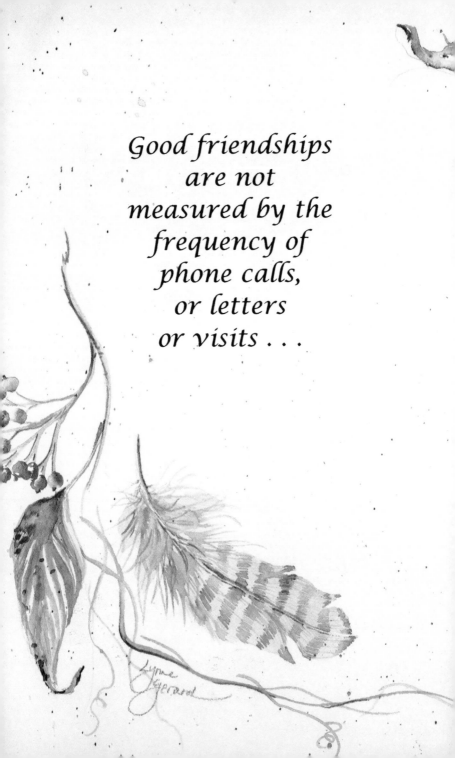

Good friendships
are not
measured by the
frequency of
phone calls,
or letters
or visits . . .

the
best
friendships
are recognised
by the quality
of
time and
feelings
shared.

Friendships
grow deeper as
trust and
co-operation
evolve from
shared
experiences . . .

Lynne
Gerard

There is a place,
between friends,
for
seriousness
as well as humour,
and countless
ways to
show appreciation.

Time passes by
and steals the
days and years.
Changes are
many, and often . . .
they always will
be . . . but a good
friendship lasts
a lifetime.